## For the Teacher

This reproducible study guide consists of instructional material to use in conjunction with the novel *To Kill a Mockingbird*. Written in chapter-by-chapter format, the guide contains a synopsis, pre-reading activities, vocabulary and comprehension exercises, as well as extension activities to be used as follow-up to the novel.

NOVEL-TIES are either for whole class instruction using a single title or for group instruction where each group uses a different novel appropriate to its reading level. Depending upon the amount of time allotted to it in the classroom, each novel, with its guide and accompanying lessons, may be completed in two to four weeks.

The first step in using NOVEL-TIES is to distribute to each student a copy of the novel and a folder containing all of the duplicated worksheets. Begin instruction by selecting several pre-reading activities in order to set the stage for the reading ahead. Vocabulary exercises for each chapter always precede the reading so that new words will be reinforced in the context of the book. Use the questions on the chapter worksheets for class discussion or as written exercises.

The benefits of using NOVEL-TIES are numerous. Students read good literature in the original, rather than in abridged or edited form. The good reading habits formed by practice in focusing on interpretive comprehension and literary techniques will be transferred to the books students read independently. Passive readers become active, avid readers.

*Novel-Ties® are printed on recycled paper.*

## SYNOPSIS

*To Kill a Mockingbird* is the story of a middle-class white family in a small Southern town who become involved in a divisive racial trial. The novel begins with a family history narrated by Jean Louise Finch, whose nickname is "Scout." Descended from landed Southern gentry, the current Finch family are now professionals in Maycomb, Alabama. Scout's father Atticus has a fairly successful law practice. They live with Jem, Scout's older brother, and the family cook Calpurnia, an African-American woman. Mrs. Finch died when Scout was two.

Scout and her brother Jem are friends with Dill Harris, a boy who visits each summer from Meridian, Mississippi. The three children spend all of their time together. They are fascinated with the Radley place because it has been the subject of town gossip and superstition. Boo Radley got into legal trouble fifteen years earlier and his father took custody of him within their house. The children want to entice Boo Radley out of seclusion.

In the fall, Dill returns to Mississippi, and Scout begins her first year at school. It is a total disappointment to her because Miss Caroline, her teacher, appreciates neither her ability to read nor her rational explanation for her classmate Walter Cunningham's pride. Although Scout would prefer to stay home and be educated by her father, she agrees to a bargain he offers her: he will continue to read to her nightly provided she returns to school and promises not to tell her teacher about it.

Toward the end of the school year, Scout notices chewing gum and then a box of pennies in the knot of the oak tree at the Radley place. She presumes they are left as gifts for her. A long-time neighbor, Miss Maudie Atkinson, tries to dispel some of the terrible myths that have grown up around Boo Radley. With their curiosity aroused, the three children sneak out at night to peak into the Radley house, but a shotgun blast in their direction frightens them off. The next year the gifts continue to be left in the knothole, but after Jem and Scout leave a "thank you note," they find the hole has been cemented closed.

Despite Maycomb's narrow-minded bigotry, Atticus Finch decides to serve as defense lawyer for Tom Robinson, a black man who is a member of Calpurnia's church. He has been wrongly accused of raping a white woman, Mayella Ewell. As a result of their father's action, Scout and Jem face derision at school, at a family Christmas celebration at Finch's Landing, and around town. In retaliation for her racist statements, Jem destroys Mrs. Dubose's flower garden. Atticus punishes Jem by making him apologize to her and read to her daily for a month. When she dies shortly thereafter, it is learned that she had been a morphine addict. Jem's reading had distracted her, helping her effort to break her drug addiction before she died.

A visit to Calpurnia's church introduces Scout and Jem to the separate world of Maycomb's African-American citizens. The children are saddened to learn that a collection is being made for Tom Robinson's wife because no white family will hire her ever since Tom was accused of the crime.

During the summer, Aunt Alexandra comes to live with the Finches in order to supervise the household once the trial begins. Her preoccupation with their family background and her displeasure with the children's visits to Calpurnia's church are sources of mutual irritation. Dill, who feels like an outcast in his own home since his mother remarried, seeks refuge in the Finch home for the summer. He receives permission to stay until school begins.

As the trial approaches, the pace of the story accelerates. Atticus is physically threatened by local townspeople for his defense of Tom Robinson. On the opening day of the trial, Maycomb is swarming with people. Disobeying Atticus's instructions, Jem, Scout, and Dill attend the beginning of the trial where they observe Atticus trying to prove that Mayella Ewell was assaulted by her own father, not Tom Robinson. Furthermore, since Tom had lost the use of one good arm years ago, it would have been difficult for him to rape a strong country girl.

Despite Atticus's excellent defense, the jury convicts Tom. The town's African-American citizens, however, show their appreciation to Atticus for his dedication to Tom's cause by leaving many gifts of food at his home. But Atticus has shown Bob Ewell to be a liar, and in retaliation, Ewell threatens to kill Atticus.

Late in August it is learned that Tom Robinson was shot trying to escape prison. Predictably, most of the townspeople react indifferently.

On Halloween night, as Jem and Scout are walking home from school, they are attacked suddenly by Bob Ewell. When the sheriff arrives, however, he finds that Ewell is lying dead under the oak tree. Ironically, the children have been saved by Boo Radley, the man whom the town feared most.

## BACKGROUND INFORMATION

Two centuries of slavery shaped attitudes and values that persist in our society. After the Civil War, there was a short period of time when African Americans participated in forming new state governments and were treated with equality under the law. Their hunger to learn caused them to start their own schools and adult education centers. These years, however, were cut short during President Andrew Johnson's term of office. Eager to be reconciled with Southern states, he pardoned former Souther politicians who had fought against the Union and delivered power into the hands of the white supremacists, giving tacit approval to groups like the Ku Klux Klan. A wave of terror spread throughout the South. Blacks who had moved into positions of influence, or who were assisting their own people to gain economic independence, were threatened and killed. There was no justice for black people in Southern courts; many were imprisoned and sentenced to hard labor on manufactured charges or for minor infractions.

Blacks were segregated in all public and private places. The 1896 Plessy *vs.* Ferguson Supreme Court ruling upheld the concept of "separate but equal" railroad accommodations and education for blacks and whites. There were separate schools for black children, separate entrances to stores and public buildings, and black people were required to ride in the back seats of streetcars and buses. Each state developed its own voting qualifications, and some charged a poll tax, which had the effect of denying to black men the right to vote.

With no economic base or political strength, and subject to the terror of white supremacists, African Americans in the South after the Civil War were hardly better off than they were before. A Federal government, now eager to repair the damages to a country split apart by the Civil War, mainly ignored the plight of former slaves. This system of oppression, promoted and tolerated by Southern state governments, remained unchanged until the late 1950s when liberal Northerners of all races joined the Southern blacks to organize for the civil rights of the entire nation.

## PRE-READING ACTIVITIES AND DISCUSSION QUESTIONS

1.  Preview the book by reading the title and the author's name and by looking at the illustration on the cover of the book. Also, read the publisher's blurb on the paperback cover or book jacket. What do you think the title signifies? When and where does the book take place?

2.  **Social Studies Connection:** Read the Background Information on page two of this study guide and do some additional research to find out more about the following topics:

    - Reconstruction era

    - Jim Crow laws

    - Poll tax

    - Ku Klux Klan

    - Plessy *vs.* Ferguson (Supreme Court ruling 1896)

    - Brown *vs.* Board of Education of Topeka (Supreme Court ruling 1954)

3.  Try to obtain photographs showing life in a small, rural Southern town in the 1930s. Notice the architecture, the clothing people wore, and the activities they engaged in. Display the photographs on a class bulletin board.

4.  In this novel, the townspeople are unfriendly toward a man whom they consider strange. Why do people dislike and distrust those who are different from them? Have you ever seen examples of this attitude?

5.  Invite a lawyer into class, or interview one on your own. To get a better perspective on the challenges the lawyer in this book faces, speak to a criminal lawyer or a civil rights lawyer. Ask this person how the legal system is set up to protect the civil rights of individuals and how this system has been compromised historically and at the present time. Also, ask the lawyer to discuss how a jury reaches its verdict in a criminal proceeding.

6.  **Cooperative Learning Activity:** Work with a small group of your classmates to consider the quotation by Charles Lamb at the beginning of the book, "Lawyers, I suppose were children once." Brainstorm to determine as many possible meanings for this quotation as you can. Conjecture on how this may be relevant to the book you are about to read.

7.  The word "precocious" means unusually advanced in mental development. Scout, one of the central characters in this novel, is a precocious child who often suffers because of her precocity. Why do you think a child may have problems with teachers, parents, other adults, or peers because he or she is advanced? Have you or anyone you know ever faced this problem?

## CHAPTER 1

**Vocabulary:** Use the context to help you choose the best meaning for the underlined word in each of the following sentences. Then circle the letter of the definition you choose.

1. The pain in my injured arm was <u>assuaged</u> by resting it and applying a topical anesthetic.

   a. deciphered          b. completed          c. relieved          d. impressed

2. My <u>predilection</u> for solitude made my neighbors think I was unfriendly.

   a. forecast          b. dilemma          c. event          d. inclination

3. My <u>taciturn</u> sister married her opposite—an outgoing, talkative young man.

   a. quiet          b. aggressive          c. hostile          d. drowsy

4. Once the temperature reached ninety degrees, it took a great effort even to <u>amble</u> across the square.

   a. walk quickly          b. walk slowly          c. skip          d. skate

5. The linen flapping on the line to dry outside appeared to be a <u>phantom</u> floating toward our house.

   a. beneficiary          b. illusion          c. vicious warrior          d. alien visitor

**Questions:**

1. Why were the children fascinated with the Radley house? What was the first "dare" they made concerning the house?

2. How did the Radley house acquire its reputation? Do you think it was a deserved reputation?

3. How did the Finches originally come to Montgomery? What was the "disturbance between the North and the South"?

4. Compare and contrast Dill's family situation with Scout's.

5. What evidence showed that Scout was a bright little girl?

**Questions for Discussion:**

1. Would you like to live in a town like Maycomb, Alabama? What would be the advantages and disadvantages of living in this small town?

2. What do you think about the children's goal to make Boo Radley come out? Was it a cruel activity or just a game?

## Chapter 1 (cont.)

**Literary Devices:**

I. *Exposition*—Exposition refers to the background information which the reader requires to understand the actions and motivations of the characters. Reread the first four pages of the book and record what you learned about the setting, the main characters, and the beginnings of a plot conflict in a chart, such as the one below.

| | |
|---|---|
| **Setting –** Maycomb | |
| **Characters:** Scout Jem Dill Atticus Calpurnia | |
| **Plot –** Conflict | |

II. *Point of View*—Point of view in literature refers to the voice telling the story. It could be the author as narrator or one of the characters in the story.

Who is telling the story?

_____

Is it being told as it happens or as a memory of times past?

_____

How does this point of view affect the actions witnessed by the reader and the language used in the narrative?

_____

_____

**Writing Activity:**

Write about a person you know whose reputation does or does not reflect his or her true personality. Tell how the reputation affects this person's life.

## CHAPTERS 2, 3

**Vocabulary:** Draw a line from each word on the left to its definition on the right. Then use the numbered words to fill in the blanks in the sentences below.

1. tranquil                a. act of conducting business
2. inequities              b. annoyances
3. fractious               c. able to read and write
4. disapprobation          d. humiliation
5. mortification           e. unfair circumstances
6. vexations               f. irritable
7. transaction             g. calm
8. literate                h. disapproval

. . . . . . . . . . . . . . . . . . . . . . . . . . . . . . . . . . . . . . . . . . . . . . . .

1. It is unusual for a child to be _____ before starting school.

2. The _____ young man caused displeasure to everyone around him.

3. Racial segregation caused educational _____.

4. His _____ was confirmed by a shake of his head and a frown.

5. A signed contract was the end product of our _____ .

6. Delayed trains and crowded subways were our daily _____.

7. Her _____ was increased by the teasing of her classmates.

8. A(n) _____ day at the seashore was spoiled when a thunderstorm made us rush indoors.

## Questions:

1. Why was Scout's first day at school a terrible disappointment to her? Why did she continue to be bored?

2. Why did Scout tell Miss Caroline about Walter Cunningham?

3. What evidence indicated that Atticus, in contrast to Miss Caroline, had respect for Walter's country manners?

4. What advice about human nature did Atticus give to Scout?

## Chapters 2, 3 (cont.)

### Questions for Discussion

1. Do you remember how you learned to read? Was it automatic as Scout recalled, or can you recall the instruction you had? Do you agree with Miss Caroline that parents should not instruct their own children?

2. Why do you think Miss Caroline seemed distraught after punishing Scout?

3. What do you think of Atticus's bargain with Scout concerning their "illicit" reading? Is it a way of teaching Scout to be dishonest or a practical necessity?

### Literary Element: Characterization

Use the Venn diagram below to show the similarities and differences between the Cunningham family and the Ewell family. Record their similarities in the overlapping part of the circles.

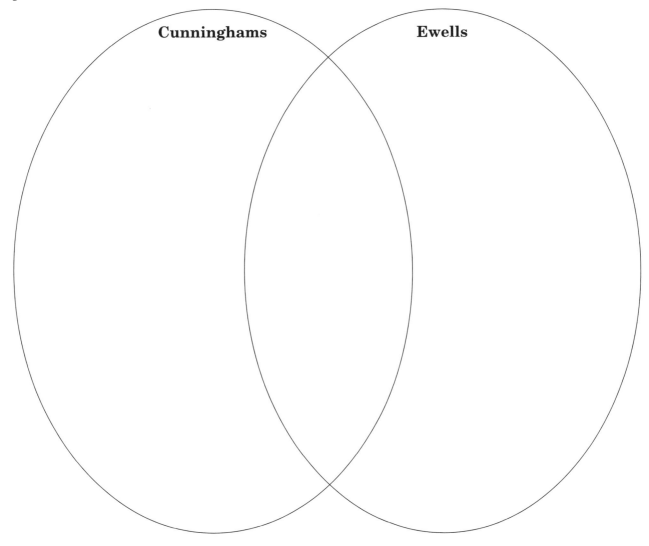

**Cunninghams**          **Ewells**

## Chapters 2, 3 (cont.)

**Literary Device: Satire**

Satire in literature is the ridicule of any subject, idea, person, or institution. How was the institution of education satirized in this book?

_____

_____

_____

_____

Do you think the author used satire in order to suggest serious reform or to gently poke fun at teachers and the educational system? Explain.

_____

_____

_____

_____

**Writing Activity:**

Imagine that you are Miss Caroline after the first day at your new teaching job in Maycomb. Write a letter to your family in northern Alabama describing what happened and how you feel about the events of the day.

## CHAPTERS 4 – 6

**Vocabulary:** Use the context to determine the meaning of the underlined word in each of the following sentences. Then check your definition with a dictionary definition.

1. The last year of high school was no more <u>auspicious</u> for my class than the first, as not a single one of my classmates was attending a college of first choice.

   Your definition _____

   Dictionary definition _____

2. The jury spent weeks deliberating in an attempt to reach a <u>unanimous</u> decision.

   Your definition _____

   Dictionary definition _____

3. In order to stay healthy, try to make a good breakfast part of your morning <u>ritual</u>.

   Your definition _____

   Dictionary definition _____

4. The soldier recounted how his <u>anxiety</u> increased the closer he came to the active battlefield.

   Your definition _____

   Dictionary definition _____

5. AIDS is a modern-day <u>pestilence</u> that is perhaps as devastating as the bubonic plague that wiped out entire populations during the Middle Ages.

   Your definition _____

   Dictionary definition _____

6. All family photographs and important documents were hidden away from the eyes of <u>inquisitive</u> visitors.

   Your definition _____

   Dictionary definition _____

7. I posted a warning sign on the tree near my wooded property for the <u>edification</u> of those who thought they might hunt there.

   Your definition _____

   Dictionary definition _____

## Chapters 4 – 6 (cont.)

**Dialect:** Southern dialect is used extensively in this novel to provide a more authentic portrayal of the rural Southern town of Maycomb. Rewrite each of the following examples of Southern dialect as standard speech.

1. Looks like if Mr. Arthur was hankerin' after heaven he'd come out on the porch at least.

   _____

   _____

2. Gracious child, I was raveling a thread, wasn't even thinking about your father.

   _____

   _____

3. "Yawl write, hear?" he bawled after us.

   _____

   _____

**Questions:**

1. How did the children amuse themselves during Dill's second summer in Maycomb? If you were their parents, would you allow them to play this game?

2. How did Jem and Dill cause Scout to become closer to Miss Maudie? What message was she trying to convey to Scout about Boo Radley?

3. Why do you think the neighbors concluded that a black person had been in Mr. Radley's collard patch?

4. Why was Jem willing to risk danger and ignore Scout's warning in order to retrieve his pants?

**Questions for Discussion:**

1. How do you think the gum and the pennies got into the knothole in the oak tree? Do you think they were meant for someone special or that the tree was someone's hiding place?

2. Why do you think Scout characterized school as "twelve years of unrelieved boredom"? What kind of schooling might have made her happier?

3. What was Scout referring to when she stated after Jem retrieved the tire, "There was more to it than he knew, but I decided not to tell him"? Why wouldn't Scout share this with Jem?

## Chapters 4 – 6 (cont.)

4. Why did Jem, Scout, and Dill think Miss Maudie was their friend despite the generation gap? Do you have any adult friend other than a relative? What makes this person special to you?

5. Why do you think Dill fabricated so many stories about himself and his father?

**Writing Activity:**

Notice how the author, Harper Lee, used language to intensify the mood of terror and suspense as Jem trespassed on the Radley property. Fill in the chart below with examples of each of the senses which Lee evoked.

| Sight | |
|-------|--|
| Sound | |
| Smell | |
| Taste | |
| Touch | |

Describe a time when you were very frightened. Use language that evokes all of your senses to recreate the feeling of terror that you experienced.

## CHAPTERS 7, 8

**Vocabulary:** Word analogies are equations in which the first pair of words has the same relationship as the second pair of words. For example: AGREE is to OBJECT as COMIC is to TRAGIC. Both pairs of words are opposites. Choose the best word from the Word Box to complete each of the analogies below.

```
                        WORD BOX
        aberrations     breeches      perplexity
        adjacent        meditative    vigil
```

1. NOZZLE is to HYDRANT as _____ is to SUIT.

2. FEEBLE is to WEAK as _____ is to CONTEMPLATIVE.

3. SENTRY is to _____ as CLERGYMAN is to PRAYER.

4. _____ is to CERTAINTY as GRIM is to JOYOUS.

5. ABNORMALITIES is to _____ as DELETE is to OMIT.

6. UNFATHOMABLE is to COMPREHENSIBLE as _____ is to DISTANT.

**Questions:**

1. What new objects did Scout and Jem find in the Radley Oak? Why were the children certain that the trinkets were for them?

2. Why did Scout fear the world was coming to an end?

3. What did Atticus mean when he said to Jem, "You've perpetrated a near libel here in the front yard"?

4. Why did Jem confess to Atticus about the children's activities regarding Boo Radley?

5. Why did Atticus decide not to have the children return Boo Radley's blanket?

6. What was Miss Maudie's reaction to the loss of her house? What did this reveal about her character?

## Chapters 7, 8 (cont.)

### Questions for Discussion:

1. Who do you think folded and sewed Jem's pants? What does this suggest to you about the person who may have done this?

2. Why do you think Jem and Scout were devastated when they found that the knothole in the oak tree had been cemented shut?

3. Why do you think Boo Radley covered Scout as she watched the fire?

### Literary Device: Simile

A simile is a figure of speech in which two unlike objects are compared using the words "like" or "as." For example:

Smoke was rolling off our house like fog off a river bank.

What is being compared?_____

What does this tell you about the smoke and the fire at Miss Maudie's house?

_____

_____

_____

### Writing Activity:

The character of Jeremy Finch is developed in the first seven chapters of the book. Review these chapters with Jem in mind. Take notes in the chart below and use these notes to write a character sketch of Jem.

**Jem**

| | |
|---|---|
| What motivates him | |
| How others react to him | |
| How he reacts to others | |
| How he reacts to situations | |

## CHAPTERS 9 – 11

**Vocabulary:** Draw a line from each word on the left to its definition on the right. Then use the numbered words to fill in the blanks in the sentences below.

1. rectitude
2. guilelessness
3. obstreperous
4. rudiments
5. mausoleum
6. articulate
7. contemporary
8. cantankerous

a. of the current age
b. first principles of a subject
c. sincerity; straightforwardness
d. large, magnificent tomb
e. unruly; boisterous
f. quarrelsome; grouchy
g. moral virtue; rightness of principle
h. able to put one's thoughts into words

· · · · · · · · · · · · · · · · · · · · · · · · · · · · · · · · · · · · · · · · · · · · · · · · · ·

1. A lawyer must be _____ to convince a jury that his client should be acquitted.

2. You must study the _____ of football before you go out on the field to play.

3. The children were so _____ that the management asked them to leave the theatre.

4. The nation honored the general's military victories after his death by building a(n) _____ in his honor.

5. _____ furniture is usually less ornate than furniture that was popular in the early 1900s.

6. Lack of sleep will cause even the most mild-mannered person to become _____.

7. After twenty years of unselfish service to his church, no one would doubt the _____ of his motives.

8. It is refreshing to observe the _____ of young children.

## Chapters 9 – 11 (cont.)

**Questions:**

1. Although Atticus told Scout that he was "simply defending a Negro," what evidence was there that this was really not a simple case?

2. Why did Atticus accept Tom Robinson's case knowing he wouldn't be paid and that it would cause a tremendous furor?

3. Why did Uncle Jack spank Scout? Why did Atticus believe she deserved this punishment even after Jack admitted his error?

4. What kind of case was Atticus referring to when he told Jack, "I was hoping to get through life without a case of this kind"?

5. What happened to change the children's perception of their father? How did it change?

6. Why did Jem destroy Mrs. Dubose's flower garden? Do you think Jem's punishment was fair and appropriate? Explain.

7. What did Mrs. Dubose do to frighten Jem? Why did Atticus feel that Mrs. Dubose was "the bravest person I ever knew"?

**Questions for Discussion:**

1. Why do you think Harper Lee focused so much attention on the history of Atticus's family and Finch's Landing? What connection might it have to the problems the family would now have to face?

2. Knowing that he wouldn't win and that his family would suffer, do you think Atticus was right to accept Tom Robinson's case?

**Literary Device: Symbolism**

A symbol in literature refers to a tangible object that represents an abstract idea or set of ideas. Consider Mrs. Dubose's camellias and how they grew back after Jem mutilated them. What might the camellias symbolize in this novel?

_____

_____

_____

_____

## Chapters 9 – 11 (cont.)

### Literary Element: Characterization

It might be said that the events in Chapters Ten and Eleven served mainly to develop the character of Atticus. What was learned about Atticus's character in the incidents with the mad dog and Mrs. Dubose?

_____

_____

_____

_____

How might these character traits help him in the trial that faces him?

_____

_____

_____

_____

### Writing Activity:

Look back over Chapter Ten which begins with Scout's perception of her father and goes on to record how this perception changed. Think about an adult in your life and write about an event that changed or reinforced your perception of that person.

## CHAPTERS 12 – 14

**Vocabulary:** Synonyms are words with similar meanings; antonyms are words with opposite meanings. Choose words from the Word Box to fill in the chart with synonyms and antonyms for the numbered words. Then use the numbered words to fill in the blanks in the sentences below.

*WORD BOX*

| | | |
|---|---|---|
| appease | frolicsome | positive |
| appropriate | incoherent | sensible |
| contradictory | negative | strange |
| | | vex |

| | **Synonym** | **Antonym** |
|---|---|---|
| 1.  inconsistent | | |
| 2.  alien | | |
| 3.  frivolous | | |
| 4.  affirmative | | |
| 5.  antagonize | | |

1. Scout always looked forward to the _____ days of summer in contrast to the gloomy, rigidly scheduled days of winter.

2. It was typical of a twelve year old like Jem to be _____ and moody.

3. With a(n) _____ nod of her head, Aunt Alexandra indicated that she would be staying in Maycomb for the next few months.

4. Many of the townspeople thought Atticus had adopted a(n) _____ set of principles when he agreed to defend Tom Robinson.

5. Scout was warned by Atticus not to _____ her aunt as long as she was living in their house.

## Chapters 12 – 14 (cont.)

**Questions:**

1. Why did Calpurnia fuss over the children so much before taking them to First Purchase?

2. How did Calpurnia's church differ from the white people's church?

3. What did Jem and Scout learn about segregation and the inequalities between blacks and whites during their visit to Calpurnia's church?

4. What did Scout mean when she commented that Calpurnia "had a separate existence outside our household" and that she even had a "command of two languages"?

5. Why did Atticus agree with Aunt Alexandra's wish to move in for the summer? How did the children feel about this?

6. Why could it be said that "Aunt Alexandra fitted into the world of Maycomb like a hand into a glove, but never into the world of Jem and me [Scout]"? What sense of values did Aunt Alexandra try to impart to the children?

7. What was Scout referring to when she said at the end of Chapter Thirteen, "I know now what he was trying to do, but Atticus was only a man. It takes a woman to do that kind of work"?

8. Why did Dill run away from home? What was the difference between the way he perceived his relationship with his mother and the way Scout perceived her relationship with her father?

9. What evidence showed that Jem was starting to grow up and was beginning to identify with the adult world?

**Questions for Discussion:**

Scout's horizons were slowly expanding beyond the confines of her own home. What was she learning about the world at large from Dill, Aunt Alexandra, the townspeople of Maycomb, and Calpurnia? How did their values affect her own?

## Chapters 12 – 14 (cont.)

### Literary Element: Characterization

In the following short description, Harper Lee was able to provide a succinct visual image of Aunt Alexandra.

> *Enarmored, upright, uncompromising*, Aunt Alexandra was sitting in a rocking chair exactly as if she had sat there every day of her life.

The careful choice of three adjectives or descriptive words encapsulated Aunt Alexandra's appearance and character. Use the chart below to do the same thing for the other main characters in the book.

| Characters | Adjectives | | |
|---|---|---|---|
| Aunt Alexandra | enarmored | upright | uncompromising |
| Atticus | | | |
| Scout | | | |
| Jem | | | |
| Calpurnia | | | |
| Dill | | | |

### Writing Activity:

Choose someone you know and try to encapsulate his or her appearance and character in three adjectives.

| | | | |
|---|---|---|---|
| | | | |

Now incorporate these adjectives into a character sketch of that person.

## CHAPTERS 15 – 18

**Vocabulary:** Use words from the Word Box to complete the analogies below.

| WORD BOX | | | |
|---|---|---|---|
| affluent | fragile | perpetual | succinct |
| amiable | inaudible | placid | |

1. SIREN is to SHRILL as HEARTBEAT is to _____.

2. PROSPEROUS is to _____ as IMPOVERISHED is to INDIGENT.

3. BIGOTRY is to TOLERANCE as _____ is to TURBULENT.

4. GENIAL is to _____ as BRAVE is to COURAGEOUS.

5. COMMITTED is to INDIFFERENT as RAMBLING is to _____.

6. _____ is to CHRONIC as INTERMITTENT is to OCCASIONAL.

7. FRAGRANT is to FLOWERS as _____ is to GLASS.

### Questions:

1. Why did Heck Tate and the men accompanying him want Tom Robinson moved out of the local jail? Why didn't Atticus agree?

2. How did Scout diffuse the passions of the gang that met Atticus at the jail? How do you think Mr. Cunningham felt about Scout's verbal exchange with him?

3. Why did Miss Maudie complain that Maycomb looked like a Roman carnival on the day the trial began? Why were so many people in town?

4. How would you characterize the crowd that came to the trial? Why do you think the author described them in such detail?

5. What did the men in the Idlers' Club mean as they echoed town sentiment saying, "the court appointed him [Atticus] to defend this nigger . . . but Atticus plans to defend him. That's what I don't like about it"?

6. On what single issue did Atticus build his case?

7. Why did Mayella resent Atticus?

# Chapters 15 – 18 (cont.)

## Questions for Discussion:

1. Why did Scout compare the moment when Atticus stood in the middle of an empty street pushing up his glasses to the moment in the jail house when he folded his newspaper? What did these two moments and these gestures have in common? What character traits did they establish that would be echoed in the courtroom experience?

2. Why do you think the author slowed up the action of the novel during the trial scene by paying meticulous attention to every aspect of the courtroom?

3. What kinds of strategies did Atticus use with witnesses on the stand to get at the truth? Do you think he built a good case for his client Tom Robinson?

4. Who do you think will be Atticus's only witness? Explain why you reached this conclusion.

## Literary Device: Building Suspense

Everything that has occurred so far in the novel has led to the moment of the trial. How did the author use descriptions of settings and events immediately prior to the trial to build and intensify a mood of suspense?

## Writing Activity:

Imagine that you are a reporter writing a news article about the first day of Tom Robinson's trial. Describe the issue as well as the scene inside and outside the court-house. Also, include statements that might have been made by one of the men in the "Idlers' Club," Reverend Sykes, and Miss Stephanie Crawford.

## CHAPTERS 19 – 22

**Vocabulary:** Use the context to help you choose the best synonym for the underlined word in each of the following sentences.

1. He had the incredible <u>temerity</u> to challenge the policeman's right to give him a ticket.
   a. shyness      b. rashness      c. cleverness      d. stupidity

2. Beyond a certain age, children become too <u>cynical</u> to believe in Santa Claus.
   a. serious      b. trusting      c. intelligent      d. distrustful

3. The jurors had to maintain a <u>discreet</u> silence until the case was over.
   a. careful      b. foolish      c. legal      d. absurd

4. The ex-convict tried to <u>expunge</u> all evidence of former misdeeds from his records.
   a. add      b. obliterate      c. belittle      d. exaggerate

5. The cold, brisk weather <u>exhilarated</u> the walkers.
   a. invigorated      b. saddened      c. annoyed      d. tired

**Questions:**

1. Why did Scout pity Mayella even though she was testifying against Tom?

2. What was the "subtlety of Tom's predicament" on the day Mayella tried to seduce him?

3. Compare Scout's and Dill's reactions to Mr. Gilmer's prosecution. Why do you think Dill became so upset when Mr. Gilmer cross-examined Tom? Why did Dolphus Raymond believe that Dill wouldn't react so strongly when he was older?

4. Why had Dolphus Raymond made himself into a town outcast? What commentary was he making about the town and its values?

5. According to Atticus in his summation speech, what was the only way that people in this country were equal? Do you think Atticus believed this or that it was a strategy to influence the jury?

6. Why were the spectators at the trial appalled when Tom Robinson said that he felt sorry for Mayella? What did this reveal about class structure in Maycomb County?

7. Why did the author make it seem like an airtight case in Atticus's favor just prior to the jury's decision?

## Chapters 19 – 22 (cont.)

8. What did Atticus mean when he said to Aunt Alexandra, "This is their home . . . they might as well learn to cope with it . . . It's just as much Maycomb County as missionary teas."

9. Why did Miss Maudie invite the children in for cake on the day after the trial? What did she mean when she told them, "It's just a baby step, but it's a step"?

10. What evidence showed that the black community appreciated all that Atticus had done even though Tom was convicted?

### Questions for Discussion:

1. Why did Atticus allow Jem and Scout to attend the trial? Do you think they should have been there?

2. What is your assessment of the townspeople of Maycomb and the jury that convicted Tom Robinson? If you were Atticus's family, could you continue to live in Maycomb without bitterness?

### Literary Device: Foreshadowing

Foreshadowing in literature refers to the clues an author provides to indicate that an event will take place. How did Harper Lee foreshadow the guilty verdict?

_____

_____

_____

_____

### Writing Activity:

In this novel, as in life, nothing is either perfectly good or perfectly evil. It would have been easy to offer a blatant indictment of the Ewell's crime, the town's bigotry, Aunt Alexandra's narrow-mindedness, Dolphus Raymond's eccentricity, Mrs. Dubose's nastiness and drug addiction. Harper Lee, however, always counter-balanced the evil with the good in order to portray the real complexities of life. Describe in a well thought-out essay how each of these possible indictments were tempered by positive counterpoints. Why do you think the author always fell short of making outright indictments against the society being described? What do you think she was really trying to convey about the nature of bigotry and injustice?

## CHAPTERS 23 – 25

**Vocabulary:** Circle the synonym for the boldface word in each word group. Use a dictionary if necessary. Then use the boldface words to fill in the blanks in the sentences below.

| | | | |
|---|---|---|---|
| 1. **furtive** | clandestine | straightforward | forlorn |
| 2. **adamant** | unyielding | weak | eager |
| 3. **sordid** | generous | degraded | filthy |
| 4. **squalid** | glamorous | pretentious | wretched |
| 5. **brevity** | conciseness | width | length |

. . . . . . . . . . . . . . . . . . . . . . . . . . . . . . . . . . . . . . . . . . . . . . . . . .

1. _____ and accuracy are important in any summary.

2. Even the police were appalled at the _____ nature of the crime.

3. With a(n) _____ glance in the direction of the surveillance cameras, the robber grabbed the bundle of money and fled.

4. The judge was _____ in his demand that jurors keep an open mind.

5. It will take more than a coat of paint and new shrubbery to make our _____, old house seem warm and welcoming.

**Questions:**

1. How did Atticus justify Bob Ewell's provocative behavior? Why do you think he told this to the children?

2. What did Atticus mean when he told Jem that "we generally get the juries we deserve"?

3. According to Atticus, what was the difference between the Cunninghams and the Ewells? Why did Atticus select a Cunningham for the jury?

4. As a result of the conviction, what conclusions did Jem draw about Boo Radley's seclusion?

5. During the afternoon with the ladies, what was Scout coming to realize about herself when she mused, "There was no doubt about it, I must soon enter this world . . ."? However, which world did Scout still prefer?

6. What was the reaction of the majority of Maycomb County to Tom's death? Why do you think the author presented opposing points of view on the subject of Tom's death?

7. How did Mr. Underwood, in his editorial on Tom Robinson's death, evoke the symbol of the mockingbird?

## Chapters 23 – 25 (cont.)

**Questions for Discussion:**

1. How did Atticus's remark that "It's all adding up and one of these days we're going to pay the bill for it," relate to the civil rights struggles of the late 1950s and 1960s when this book was written?

2. Why do you think it was important for Aunt Alexandra and Miss Maudie to hide their sorrow at Tom's death?

**Literary Device: Irony**

Irony refers to a situation which is the opposite of what is expected. Dramatic irony refers to a situation in which the reader sees a character's mistakes or misunderstandings, which the character is unable to see.

What was the implicit irony in the Maycomb ladies' concern for the poverty and mistreatment of the Mrunas and Mrs. Merriweather's statement to Scout, "you are a fortunate girl. You live in a Christian home with Christian folks in a Christian town"?

_____

_____

_____

_____

_____

_____

**Writing Activity:**

Write about an ironic situation in your own life. Describe the situation or the event and why its outcome was unexpected. Also, indicate whether the irony caused pleasure or pain.

## Chapters 23 – 25 (cont.)

**Literary Element: Plot**

The plot of a story refers to the events in the order they occurred. *To Kill a Mockingbird* has two parallel plots—the Boo Radley story line and the Tom Robinson story line. Use the chart below to record the main events in each story line so far.

$$\boxed{\textbf{PLOT}}$$

| Making Boo Radley Come Out | Trial of Tom Robinson |
|---|---|
|  |  |

How might these two plots relate? Why do you think they were juxtaposed?

_____

_____

_____

_____

_____

_____

_____

## CHAPTERS 26 – 31

**Vocabulary:** Use the context to determine the meaning of the underlined word in each of the following sentences.

1.  Whenever Scout passed the old house, she felt a tinge of <u>remorse</u> for having teased Boo Radley.

    a.  callousness      b.  sadness      c.  repentance      d.  fear

2.  As the only man who was ever fired from the WPA for laziness, Mr. Bob Ewell was considered <u>unique</u>.

    a.  unprecedented      b.  commonplace      c.  tragic      d.  industrious

3.  Mrs. Merriweather made last-minute changes in her script as she stood at the <u>lectern</u>.

    a.  folding chair      b.  stage light      c.  reading stand      d.  brass railing

4.  No matter how hard I struggled, I was unable to release my arms, which were tightly <u>pinioned</u> against my sides.

    a.  bound      b.  filed      c.  folded      d.  muscled

5.  I nodded toward the person standing in the corner because I knew Atticus would <u>reprimand</u> me for pointing.

    a.  compliment      b.  accuse      c.  praise      d.  scold

**Questions:**

1.  What evidence indicated that the townspeople had mixed feelings about Atticus after the trial?

2.  Why was Scout upset by her teacher's indictment of Hitler? Why did Jem react so violently when Scout tried to talk to him about it?

3.  According to Atticus, why did Bob Ewell continue to hold a grudge against everyone connected with the Robinson case even though he had won in court?

4.  What misconception did Atticus have at first about the way Bob Ewell was killed? Why did Sheriff Tate want people to think Ewell fell on his own knife?

5.  What do you think Scout meant when she said that to reveal Boo Radley's part in Bob Ewell's death would be "like shootin' a mockingbird"?

# Chapters 26 – 31 (cont.)

6. What insight came to Scout as she stood on Boo Radley's porch after taking him home?

7. What message was Atticus trying to convey to his daughter at the end of the book when he said, "Most people are, Scout, when you finally see them"?

## Questions for Discussion:

1. Why do you think the author included some positive or mitigating information about Tom Ewell, rather than offering a complete moral indictment of the man?

2. What other incidents in the novel did the author present in both a positive and negative light? Why do you think she did this, instead of branding specific incidents or people as being either good or evil? Which manner of portrayal do you prefer?

3. After all that happened in Maycomb before and after the trial, can you appreciate Atticus's positive view of his community and the people in it, or do you disagree with his opinion?

## Writing Activities:

1. As Scout recalled the summer of the trial, she used the following simile to describe the time:

   . . . the events of the summer hung over us like smoke in a closed room.

   Write about a time when events in your life made you feel the same way.

2. Since Boo Radley was too shy for conversation, imagine you are Scout or Jem and write a letter to him expressing your appreciation for all he has done for you over the years. You might also allude to the times you spied on him and possibly apologize for your childish curiosity.

## CLOZE ACTIVITY

The following passage has been taken from Chapter Thirty-one of the novel. Read it through completely and then go back and fill in each blank with a word that makes sense. Then you may compare your language with that of the author.

　　　　We came to the street light on the corner, and I wondered how many times Dill had stood there hugging the fat pole, watching, waiting, hoping. I wondered how many times Jem and I had made this _____,[1] but I entered the Radley front gate _____[2] the second time in my life. Boo _____[3] I walked up the steps to the _____.[4] His fingers found the front doorknob. He _____[5] released my hand, opened the door, went inside, _____[6] shut the door behind him. I never _____[7] him again.

　　　　Neighbors bring food with death _____[8] flowers with sickness and little things in _____.[9] Boo was our neighbor. He gave us _____[10] soap dolls, a broken watch and chain, _____[11] pair of good-luck pennies, and our lives. _____[12] neighbors give in return. We never put _____[13] into the tree what we took out _____[14] it: we had given him nothing, and _____[15] made me sad.

　　　　I turned to go _____.[16] Street lights winked down the street all _____[17] way to town. I had never seen _____[18] neighborhood from this angle. There were Miss Maudie's, Miss Stephanie's—_____[19] was our house, I could see the _____[20] swing—Miss Rachel's house was beyond us, plainly _____.[21] I could even see Mrs. Dubose's.

　　　　I looked _____[22] me. To the left of the brown _____[23] was a long shuttered window. I walked _____[24] it, stood in front of it, and _____[25] around. In daylight, I thought, you could _____[26] to the postoffice corner.

　　　　Daylight . . . in my _____,[27] the night faded. It was daytime and _____[28] neighborhood was busy. Miss Stephanie Crawford crossed the street _____[29] tell the latest to Miss Rachel. Miss Maudie bent _____[30] her azaleas. It was summertime, and two _____[31] scampered down the side-walk toward a man _____[32] in the distance. The man waved, and the children raced each other to him.

## POST-READING ACTIVITIES AND DISCUSSION QUESTIONS

1.  When Harper Lee published her novel *To Kill a Mockingbird* in 1960, it appeared on the Best Seller List for eighty weeks and was chosen as a Literary Guild and Book-of-the-Month Club selection. In 1961 Harper Lee won the Pulitzer Prize for fiction. To what do you attribute this book's tremendous popular appeal and critical acclaim?

2.  During the course of a novel, some characters evolve and grow, while others remain the same, as their personalities are slowly revealed. Discuss how Scout and Jem evolve from the beginning to the end of the book. Discuss also how the reader's perception of Atticus's character changes and is enriched even though his personality stays the same.

3.  How has life in the rural South changed since the 1930s as portrayed in Harper Lee's novel? In what ways has it remained the same?

4.  Even though Harper Lee is critical of the South, it is evident that she loved her section of the country. How was this manifest in the novel?

5.  "Caste" refers to any rigid system of social distinctions. What were the various stratifications of the caste system that Harper Lee described in Maycomb County? How did caste affect the actions of the main characters in this novel?

6.  At the beginning of the novel, Jem and Scout felt fear and superstition toward the Radley and the Dubose homes as well as the inhabitants within. Describe how Jem and Scout dispelled these irrational feelings as fear and ignorance were replaced with knowledge and security.

7.  The "point of view" in a work of literature is the author's choice of who shall tell the story. Analyze how the point of view changed in the novel even while the narrator remained the same. Discuss how this novel would have been different if it were told from Atticus's point of view.

8.  Tell how the device of flashback and the story of Boo Radley served to frame the events of the entire novel.

9.  How did the Civil War and its outcome remain a part of Maycomb society in the 1930s?

## Post-Reading Activities and Discussion Questions (cont.)

10. The theme in a literary work is its controlling idea. It is the underpinning beneath the plot, the force behind the characterization. In Harper Lee's novel there is not one single theme, but many themes competing for attention and prominence. Although prejudice and bigotry are its central themes, for example, it would be too simple to suppose that this novel is just an indictment of racial prejudice in the South. Examine the following themes and discuss how each is manifest in the book:
    * loss of innocence
    * isolation and courage
    * injustice
    * integrity in the face of injustice
    * human kindness in the face of injustice
    * bravery
    * disparity between appearance and reality
    * need to walk in another person's shoes

11. View the film version of *To Kill a Mockingbird*. Do you think the actors were well cast? What changes were made between the book and the film? Why do you think these changes and omissions were made? What parts of the film appeared as you had imagined them in the book? Which version did you prefer—the book or the film?

12. **Literature Circle:** Have a literature circle discussion in which you tell your personal reactions to *To Kill a Mockingbird*. Here are some questions and sentence starters to help your literature circle begin a discussion.
    * How are you like Scout or Jem? How are you different?
    * Do you think the characters in the novel are realistic? Why or why not?
    * Which character is most like you? How?
    * Which character did you like the most? The least?
    * Who else would you like to read this novel? Why?
    * What questions would you like to ask the author about this novel?
    * It was not fair when . . .
    * I would have liked to see . . .
    * I wonder . . .
    * Scout and Jem learned that . . .

## SUGGESTIONS FOR FURTHER READING

Capote, Truman. *Other Voices Other Rooms*. Penguin.

_____. *The Grass Harp and Tree of Night and Other Short Stories*. Penguin.

\* Cleaver, Bill, and Vera Cleaver. *Where the Lilies Bloom*. HarperCollins.

\* Dickens, Charles. *Great Expectations*. Penguin.

Faulkner, William. *Light in August*. Random House.

\* Greene, Bette. *Summer of My German Soldier*. Penguin.

\* Hunt, Irene. *No Promises in the Wind*. Random House.

Lawrence, Jerome, and Robert E. Lee. *Inherit the Wind*. Random House.

_____. *The Night Thoreau Spent in Jail*. Random House.

\* Lipsyte, Robert. *The Contender*. HarperCollins.

McCullers, Carson. *Member of the Wedding*. Random House.

\* Paterson, Katherine. *Bridge to Terabithia*. HarperCollins.

\* Peck, Richard. *A Day No Pigs Would Die*. Random House.

\* Salinger, J.D. *Catcher in the Rye*. Warner.

\* Taylor, Mildred. *Let the Circle Be Unbroken*. Random House.

\* _____. *Roll of Thunder, Hear My Cry*. Random House.

\* Twain, Mark. *Adventures of Huckleberry Finn*. Random House.

\* _____. *Adventures of Tom Sawyer*. Random House.

\* Voigt, Cynthia. *Dicey's Song*. Simon & Schuster.

\* _____. *Homecoming*. Simon & Schuster.

Williams, Tennessee. *Glass Menagerie*. W.W. Norton.

\* Wright, Richard. *Black Boy*. HarperCollins.

\* Zindel, Paul. *The Pigman*. HarperCollins.

\* NOVEL-TIES Study Guides are available for these titles.

# ANSWER KEY

**Chapter 1**
Vocabulary: 1. c  2. d  3. a  4. b  5. b
Questions: 1. The Radley house, like forbidden fruit, was interesting and mysterious—myths had grown up around its inhabitants. The first dare was made during Dill's first summer in Maycomb. Dill dared Jem to go to Boo Radley's house and try to make Boo Radley come outside. 2. The Radley's had never participated in any of the town's normal activities. They had locked away their son for fifteen years. Their remoteness caused gossip and stories to abound concerning the family and the house. Answers to the second part of the question will vary. 3. The Finches were the descendants of Simon Finch, a fur trapper who settled farm land in Maycomb County. The "disturbance" was the Civil War. 4. Dill had an unhappy home situation, living with his indifferent mother and stepfather. Scout had a happy home situation, living with her brother, adoring father, and housekeeper Calpurnia. 5. We know that Scout was bright because she learned to read before she entered kindergarten.

**Chapters 2, 3**
Vocabulary: 1. g  2. e  3. f  4. h  5. d  6. b  7. a  8. c; 1. literate  2. fractious  3. inequities  4. disapprobation  5. transaction  6. vexations  7. mortification  8. tranquil
Questions: 1. Scout was excited about starting school, but her enthusiasm was dampened by her teacher. She was not pleased that Scout could read and criticized her father for teaching her. Scout continued to be bored because Miss Caroline's curriculum was too staid and conventional to take advantage of Scout's precocity. 2. Scout told Miss Caroline about Walter because she wanted to help her teacher understand his behavior so that she would not humiliate him in the future. 3. Atticus showed his respect for Walter's country manners by speaking respectfully to him about farm matters and allowing him to eat his dinner with syrup without permitting any criticism from Scout. 4. Atticus advised Scout that you could never really understand people until you tried to appreciate things from their own point of view.

**Chapters 4 – 6**
Vocabulary: 1. auspicious–favorable  2. unanimous–in complete agreement  3. ritual–established ceremonial act or routine  4. anxiety–fear; nervousness  5. pestilence–deadly or virulent epidemic  6. inquisitive–curious  7. edification–instruction for moral or intellectual benefit
Questions: 1. During Dill's second summer in Maycomb, the children amused themselves by inventing an ongoing play about the Radleys. Answers to the second part of the question will vary. 2. Jem and Dill began to exclude Scout from their activities saying she was only a girl. Scout took refuge with Miss Maudie. As both a friend and neighbor to Scout, Miss Maudie tried to contribute an adult voice of reason and restraint to the Radley mythology. She wanted Scout to treat Boo as a human being, deserving of consideration and understanding. 3. Answers may vary, but should include the idea that many of the people in this provincial Southern town had relegated blacks to the role of scapegoat. 4. It wasn't that Jem really minded getting caught and paying the consequences, but he was feeling guilty about his actions and didn't want to be identified with the act of trespassing.

**Chapters 7, 8**
Vocabulary: 1. breeches  2. meditative  3. vigil  4. perplexity  5. aberrations  6. adjacent
Questions: 1. The children found twine, a pocket watch, carved soap statues of themselves, and chewing gum in the Radley Oak. The statues were such good likenesses of themselves that the children knew the gifts were for them. 2. Scout feared the world was coming to an end because she had never seen snow before and she had just heard from Mr. Avery that when children disobey their parents, among other things, this would cause the seasons to change. Scout thought the world was coming to an end because she was feeling guilty for disobeying Atticus concerning Boo Radley. 3. When Atticus scolded the children for a libelous act, he was referring to the snowman the children made that was such a good caricature of Mr. Avery that he might be insulted and want to sue. 4. Jem was so overwrought the night of the fire and he was so astonished to learn that Boo had put the blanket on Scout's shoulder, that he could contain himself no longer. He also considered Boo a friend and worried about his safety at the hands of his brother, Nathan Radley. 5. Atticus didn't have the children return the blanket because he probably feared that Boo might suffer if his brother learned that he had given Scout a blanket on the night of the fire. 6. Miss Maudie was neither discouraged nor unhappy about the loss of her house. She told the children that she had always wanted a smaller house. This incident revealed Miss Maudie's courage and optimism.

**Chapters 9 – 11**
Vocabulary: 1. g  2. c  3. e  4. b  5. d  6. h  7. a  8. f; 1. articulate  2. rudiments  3. obstreperous  4. mausoleum  5. contemporary  6. cantankerous  7. rectitude  8. guilelessness
Questions: 1. The controversiality of the case became clear when the children at school taunted Scout, when some townspeople criticized Atticus for taking on the case, and when Atticus warned Scout not to be goaded into a fight. Atticus also expressed his concerns to his brother Jack. 2. Tom Robinson was a young black man accused of raping Mayella Ewell. Atticus was defending him because he had been appointed by the court, and he believed that everyone was entitled to a fair trial with good counsel. Also, Tom Robinson was Calpurnia's friend. 3. Jack spanked Scout because she fought with Francis. Atticus believed fighting was not a correct response in any situation. 4. Atticus was worried about the case because he understood the bigotry that existed among the people in his town and knew that this would overshadow reason; that everything would be blown out of proportion and good people would suffer. 5. The children thought that their father was too old to do anything interesting or perform heroic deeds. This perception changed when they saw him shoot the rabid dog, an act that required daring and excellent marksmanship. They now had renewed respect for Atticus who suddenly seemed courageous. 6. Jem destroyed Mrs. Dubose's flower garden because she insulted his father. Answers to the last part of the question will vary. 7. Jem was frightened by Mrs. Dubose's appearance and her uncontrollable gestures. Atticus explained that she had become a morphine addict after a long illness, and that she had just broken the habit. It was very brave of her to be willing to withstand the pain of her illness as well as the withdrawal symptoms so that she would be able to die without being beholden to the morphine.

**Chapters 12 – 14**
Vocabulary: 1. inconsistent: S–contradictory, A–incoherent  2. alien: S–strange, A–appropriate  3. frivolous: S–frolicsome, A–sensible  4. affirmative: S–positive, A–negative  5. antagonize: S–vex, A–appease; 1. frivolous  2. inconsistent  3. affirmative  4. alien  5. antagonize
Questions: 1. Since churches were segregated, it was unusual for a black person to bring white children to church. Calpurnia wanted her charges to make a good impression on her friends. 2. The parishioners at Cal's church were very poor and, therefore, the building was not decorated. Since they did not have hymn books, one congregant led in the singing of hymns. They accepted Tom Robinson's hardships as their own and took up a collection for his family. The sermon was a denunciation of specific sins. 3. Jem and Scout learned that even the legal system did not mete out equal justice. Since all power was vested in white society, a perfectly decent person like Tom Robinson's wife could not get work now that her husband had been accused of rape. 4. Cal spoke black English with her own people, and standard English at the Finch home. For the first time, Scout realized that Cal had a life of her own outside the Finch household. 5. Atticus agreed that Alexandra should move in for the summer to help the children withstand the kind of criticism they were bound to receive from Maycomb residents due to Atticus's defense of Tom. The children were distraught because their aunt was rigid and established rules for deportment that made their lives miserable. 6. Aunt Alexandra displayed the same provincialism and prejudice that was exhibited by most Maycomb residents. She tried to impart a sense of the importance of heredity and good breeding to her nephew and niece. 7. Atticus had given in to Aunt Alexandra's nagging and tried to influence Scout to attain a more feminine outlook. He was also trying to apologize for buckling under to Aunt Alexandra and to console Scout in advance for what he knew would be a difficult summer. 8. Dill ran away because he felt that his mother and new stepfather did not want him. Dill felt that his mother did not need him, whereas Scout felt assured that Atticus could not live without her. 9. Jem was beginning to interpret the adult world to Scout. He didn't want to play in childish ways and he often refused to spend time with his little sister.

**Chapters 15 – 18**
Vocabulary: 1. inaudible  2. affluent  3. placid  4. amiable  5. succinct  6. perpetual  7. fragile
Questions: 1. The men warned Atticus that if his client Tom Robinson spent the night in the county jail, he would be in danger from that "old Sarum bunch." Atticus told them that the time of the Klan and lynchings was past and his client would remain for one night in the Maycomb jail. 2. With a combination of innocence and straightforwardness, Scout totally disarmed Mr. Cunningham and broke the mood of violence that had been escalating. It momentarily destroyed the gang mentality. Answers to the second part of the question will vary. 3. Miss Maudie commented that Maycomb looked like a Roman carnival because so many people from all over the county came for the trial, motivated by a mixture of curiosity and a need for diversion. 4. Much of the crowd was unkempt, uneducated, and ill-mannered. Answers to the second part of the question will vary, but may include the idea that it showed that it would be very hard for Tom Robinson to have an unprejudiced jury and, consequently, a fair trial. 5. The men in the Idlers' Club thought Atticus should have merely gone through the motions of a defense. Instead he was conducting a

real defense. 6. In his case, Atticus was focusing on Tom's physical disability and his inability to assault Mayella in the way she described. 7. Mayella resented Atticus because he revealed that she had no friends and lived with her family in abject squalor.

**Chapters 19 – 22**
Vocabulary: 1. b  2. d  3. a  4. b  5. a
Questions: 1. Scout pitied Mayella because she was a misfit in every part of Maycomb society. 2. Tom did not want to acquiesce to Mayella's overtures, but he knew that if he pushed her away he could be accused of assault. The only other alternative was to run away which made him look guilty anyway. 3. Scout was objective about Mr. Gilmer's prosecution, while Dill became so upset that he cried. Dill was upset about Mr. Gilmer's insensitive treatment of Tom. Perhaps Dill identified with this kind of treatment. Dolphus Raymond felt that children were the only ones who had the ability to react with sensitivity. Once they grew up they either became prejudiced themselves or ignored the sad truth of life in Maycomb. 4. Dolphus made himself an outcast because he rejected the mores of the South. As an outcast he was able to live the way he wanted without being bothered by the townspeople. 5. According to Atticus there was only equality in the courts. Since Southern courts in 1935 did not mete out equal justice, Atticus was probably trying to convince the jury to act judiciously, rather than out of prejudice. 6. The townspeople resented a black man feeling sorry for a white woman. In their class system any black person was inferior to any white person. 7. Making it look like an airtight case in favor of the defense made the guilty verdict seem more tragic because it was unexpected and it emphasized the injustice of the verdict. 8. Atticus meant that the children had to learn about the existence of deep-rooted prejudice against blacks in Maycomb. 9. Miss Maudie wanted to reassure the children that their father had done a fine job even though he lost the case. She wanted them to know that their values were admirable. The "baby step" was the fact that the jury had deliberated for so long. Although they had eventually handed down a verdict of guilty, it was obviously difficult for them to do so. She thought this represented progress. 10. The black onlookers in the courthouse all rose in respect for Atticus as he left the court room. The following day they sent him generous gifts of homemade food.

**Chapters 23 – 25**
Vocabulary: 1. furtive–clandestine  2. adamant–unyielding  3. sordid–degraded  4. squalid–wretched
5. brevity–conciseness; 1. brevity  2. sordid  3. furtive  4. adamant  5. squalid
Questions: 1. Atticus told the children that Bob Ewell had spit at him in order to dissipate all of his anger. Atticus didn't want the children to worry that his life was in danger. 2. Atticus explained that if responsible, reasonable adults would not accept jury duty as a responsibility, they deserved to have the task left to ignorant people. 3. According to Atticus, the Cunninghams had some sense of justice and pride, whereas the Ewells had none. Also, Scout may have reawakened the Cunningham sense of pride and justice during that night at the jail. Atticus thought that a Cunningham might sway the rest of the jury. 4. Jem decided that Boo Radley stayed at home because he did not like the world of Maycomb with its narrowmindedness and prejudice. 5. Scout realized that one day she would have to enter the feminine society of Maycomb. She wanted, however, to remain a tomboy and still preferred the straightforward company of men. 6. Most of Maycomb sustained interest in Tom's death for only two days. Mr. Underwood wrote indignantly of his senseless killing. Answers to the second part of the question will vary. 7. Mr. Underwood compared Tom Robinson's death to the senseless killing of songbirds by hunters. This related to the image of the mockingbird, referred to earlier in the book, when Jem and Scout were warned not to kill songbirds.

**Chapters 26 – 31**
Vocabulary: 1. c  2. a  3. c  4. a  5. d
Questions: 1. The townspeople seemed to instruct their children that Jem and Scout were not guilty of having Atticus as a parent. Their disappointment in Atticus was tempered, however, by electing him to the state legislature. 2. The teacher felt that Hitler treated the Jews unjustly, but did not appreciate the fact that the citizens of Maycomb treated the blacks unjustly. Jem did not want to be reminded of the day in court. 3. Despite winning the case, Ewell felt publicly humiliated. He realized that few people in Maycomb believed his story and his family's squalid life had been aired in public. 4. Atticus thought that Jem had killed Ewell. The Sheriff wanted people to think that Ewell fell on his own knife in order to spare Arthur Radley, who was too painfully shy to withstand the publicity. 5. Like a mockingbird, Arthur did good things but wanted nothing in return. Finding himself in the limelight after all these years as a recluse would be tantamount to death. 6. Scout felt that Arthur had given, but had gotten nothing back in return. 7. Atticus believed in the essential goodness of people. He felt there was good in most people, but you had to get to know them well in some cases in order to find it.